A DAY IN THE LIFE OF A COMMUNITY SERVICE VEHICLE

A DAY IN THE LIFE OF A TRACTOR

by Mae Respicio

PEBBLE
a capstone imprint

Published by Pebble, an imprint of Capstone
1710 Roe Crest Drive, North Mankato, Minnesota 56003
capstonepub.com

Copyright © 2025 by Capstone. All rights reserved. No part of this publication may be reproduced in whole or in part, or stored in a retrieval system, or transmitted in any form or by any means, electronic, mechanical, photocopying, recording, or otherwise, without written permission of the publisher.

Library of Congress Cataloging-in-Publication Data is available on the Library of Congress website.
ISBN: 9780756587147 (hardcover)
ISBN: 9780756587093 (paperback)
ISBN: 9780756587109 (ebook PDF)

Summary: A farmer gets into a huge tractor. The tractor is ready to begin a long day of work! What parts do these vehicles have? What kind of work do they do in fields and other places? Discover how tractors are used from sunrise to sunset.

Editorial Credits
Editor: Carrie Sheely; Designer: Elyse White; Media Researcher: Jo Miller; Production Specialist: Tori Abraham

Image Credits
Getty Images: ae-photos, 12, SlavkoSereda, 19, tap10, 16, Westend61, 5; Shutterstock: Hristo Uzunov, cover (front and back), Alexandr Makarov, 20 (glue), Anton Starikov, 21 (buttons), BONDART PHOTOGRAPHY, 9, CameraCraft, 7, Cliff Day, 21 (pipe cleaners), jan kranendonk, 15, Luce Morin, 4, M_Agency, 18, MyraMyra, 8, New Africa, 20 (paper), oticki, 11, SALMONNEGRO-STOCK, 14, smereka, 17, YuRi Photolife, 13

Any additional websites and resources referenced in this book are not maintained, authorized, or sponsored by Capstone. All product and company names are trademarks™ or registered® trademarks of their respective holders.

Printed and bound in China. 6097

TABLE OF CONTENTS

Helpers on the Farm 4
Ready to Work 6
Chores and More 14
The Day Is Done 18
      Tractor Artwork 20
      Glossary 22
      Read More 23
      Internet Sites 23
      Index 24
      About the Author 24

Words in **bold** are in the glossary.

HELPERS ON THE FARM

Rumble! Chug! A big tractor pulls a plow in a field. The **soil** on top is flipped over. This helps get the soil ready for planting.

A tractor pulling a plow

A tractor with equipment to collect an apple crop

Tractors are strong machines. They come in different sizes. Tractors help farmers with their work. They help farmers grow **crops**. This helps bring food to our tables. That's an important job for our **communities!**

READY TO WORK

It's a sunrise start on the farm. There's no sleeping in today! The tractor is about to have a big day.

The farmer checks the tractor. Does it have enough **fuel** and oil? Do the lights work? Do the tires have the right air **pressure**? Everything looks good!

ON THE MOVE

Today is planting day! The farmer attaches a planter behind the tractor. The tractor heads to the field. Its tires have bumps and grooves called **tread**. They help the tractor move through the loose dirt.

Tread

A tractor with a planter

The tractor travels slowly in straight lines. The planter digs the soil to **sow** the seeds. It drops in the seeds. Then it covers them with soil. Now the farmer will wait a few weeks for seeds to **sprout**.

The tractor has more work to do on the farm. The farmer attaches a bucket to the tractor's front. It is like a big scoop. The farmer controls the bucket from the **cabin**.

Tractor spreading manure on field

The bucket scoops up **manure**. The manure dumps into a spreader. Later, the farmer spreads the manure on a field. This will help the crops grow.

CHORES AND MORE

The tractor has been working hard all day. The farmer takes a short break. The tractor does too. Its engine cools. Then the farmer's cell phone rings.

A neighbor's tractor has broken down! The farmer drives the tractor over to help. Now the neighbor can get their hay wagons home before it rains.

It's near the end of the day. It's time for **chores**!

Moo! The **cattle** are hungry. It's dinnertime. What do they get? Hay! The tractor uses a bale spear. It's like a giant fork. It carries bundles of hay to the animals.

THE DAY IS DONE

As the sun sets, the tractor returns to the shed. The farmer and the tractor worked hard today.

The sky is getting darker. The tractor is done for the day. It will help again tomorrow.

TRACTOR ARTWORK

You've learned all about tractors on the farm. Now it's time to make your own!

What You Need:

- sheet of paper
- pencil
- colored pencils, pens, or crayons
- glitter, buttons, or pipe cleaners
- glue or glue stick

What You Do:

1. Look at the pictures in this book. Decide what you want your tractor to look like and what job it will be doing. Will it pull something? Will it use a bucket?

2. Draw your tractor on a sheet of paper.

3. What is your tractor doing? Add your tractor's job into the drawing.

4. Color your picture with colored pencils, pens, or crayons. Use glitter, pipe cleaners, or buttons to decorate your picture too. Share it with your friends and family to show them what you've learned.

GLOSSARY

cabin (KA-buhn)—the enclosed part of a tractor where the driver sits

chore (CHOR)—a job that has to be done regularly

community (kuh-MYOO-nuh-tee)—a group of people who live in the same area

crop (KROP)—plants grown in large amounts, usually for food

manure (muh-NUR)—waste from animals that are kept on farms

pressure (PRESH-ur)—the force produced by pressing on something

soil (SOYL)—dirt or earth in which plants grow

sow (SOH)—to plant seeds

sprout (SPRAUT)—to start to grow and produce shoots or buds

tread (TRED)—a series of bumps and deep grooves on a tire

READ MORE

Murray, Laura K. *Why Do We Need Soil?* North Mankato, MN: Capstone, 2024.

Ransom, Candice. *Go, Go, Tractors!* New York: Random House, 2021.

Rawson, Katherine. *Can Robots Milk Cows?: Questions and Answers About Farm Machines.* North Mankato, MN: Capstone, 2023.

INTERNET SITES

5 Different Types of Tractor
northeastag.com.au/5-different-types-of-tractors

John Deere for Kids
deere.com/en/connect-with-john-deere/john-deere-kids

Kiddle: Tractor Facts for Kids
kids.kiddle.co/Tractor

INDEX

bale spears, 16
buckets, 12, 13
cabin, 12
crops, 5, 13
fuel, 6

hay, 15, 16
lights, 6
manure, 13
oil, 6

planters, 8, 10
plows, 4
seeds, 10
soil, 4, 10
tires, 6, 8

ABOUT THE AUTHOR

Mae Respicio is a nonfiction writer and award-winning author of novels including *How to Win a Slime War*. Mae lives with her family in California, but the first time she ever got a ride on a tractor was on her favorite farm in Ohio.